JOHANN PACHELBEL

The Fugues on the Magnificat for Organ or Keyboard

Edited by Hugo Botstiber and Max Seiffert

Dover Publications, Inc.
New York

PUBLISHER'S NOTE

Johann Pachelbel (1653–1706), one of the major keyboard composers of the late seventeenth century and a link between the southern and central German schools, having studied in Vienna and finally settled in his native Nuremberg, composed these Magnificat fugues while organist of St. Sebald, Nuremberg's wealthiest church, where he was employed from 1695 on.

Unlike many other organ settings of the Magnificat (Canticle of the Virgin) that treated alternate verses of the chant, in the tradition of Renaissance vocal settings, Pachelbel's Magnificat fugues are preludial in nature, like his fugues based on chorales; they are brief intonations to establish the pitch for the singers, and thus occur in the contemporary equivalent of the eight different "tones" or modes of plainchant. Only a minority of them, however, use the chant formula, the majority being based on freely invented themes.

Among the 95 works in this volume (the original German title *94 Kompositionen* merely represented a miscount; nothing has been omitted or added here) are many that do not require the use of an organ pedal and can be played on other keyboard instruments.

The words "Für zwey Claviere" on page 44 mean "for two manuals." On page 99, "Rückpositiv" refers to the second main organ manual; "Oberwerk," to the upper chest and manual.

This Dover edition, first published in 1986, contains all the music from *94* [sic] *Kompositionen: Fugen über das Magnificat für Orgel oder Klavier*, as reprinted in 1959 by the Akademische Druck- u. Verlagsanstalt, Graz [Austria], from the Artaria, Vienna, edition of 1901, which was part of the serial publication *Denkmäler der Tonkunst in Österreich* (Band 17, Jahrgang VIII/2). The Publisher's Note is a new feature, specially prepared for the present edition.

The publisher is grateful to Queens College (Aaron Copland School of Music and Paul Klapper Library) for making their Pachelbel volume available for direct offset photography.

Manufactured in the United States of America
Dover Publications, Inc., 31 East 2nd Street, Mineola, N.Y. 11501

Library of Congress Cataloging-in-Publication Data

Pachelbel, Johann, 1653–1706.
   [Magnificatfugen]
   The fugues on the Magnificat.

   Reprint. Originally published: Wien : Artaria, 1901 (Denkmäler der tonkunst in Österreich ; v. 17).
   1. Canons, fugues, etc. (Organ)   I. Botstiber, Hugo.   II. Seiffert, Max.
M10.P   85-753678
ISBN 0-486-25037-7

CONTENTS

Magnificat primi toni.

I. 2.

I. 3.

I. 4.

I. 5.

I. 6.

I. 9.

I. 10.

I. 11.

(Ped.)

I. 12.

(Ped.)

I. 13.

I. 14.

I. 15.

I. 17.

I. 18.

(Ped.)

I. 19.

I. 20.

(Ped.)

I. 21.

I. 22.

Magnificat secundi toni.

II. 2.

II. 3.

II.4.

(Ped.)

II. 5.

II. 6.

(Ped.)

(Ped.)

II. 7.

(Ped.)

II. 9.

II. 10.

(Ped.)

Magnificat tertii toni.

III. 3.

III. 4.

III. 5.

III. 6.

III. 7.

Für zwey Claviere.

III. 8.

III. 9.

Magnificat quarti toni.

IV. 5.

IV. 6.

(Ped.)

IV. 7.

Magnificat quinti toni.

V. 1.

(Ped.

V. 2.

V. 3.

V. 6.

V. 9.

V. 11.

Magnificat sexti toni.

VI. 3.

VI. 6.

(Ped.)

VI. 8.

(Ped.)

Magnificat septimi toni.

VII. 5.

Magnificat octavi toni.

VIII. 1.

(Ped.)

(Ped.)

VIII.4.

VIII. 7.

VIII.8.

(Ped.)

VIII. 9.

VIII.11.